Whales belong to the order cetacea, which means that they are mammals fully adapted to aquatic life. Whales are one of the most amazing creatures that live in the planet. They inhabit all oceans of the world.

Whales are large, intelligent, aquatic mammals. Whales breathe via blowholes; baleen whales have two and toothed whales have one.

They are the only mammals, other than manatees, that live their entire lives in the water, and the only mammals that have adapted to life in the open oceans.

Whales are descendants of land-living animals which returned to water after living millions of years in land.

There are two
types of whales
that are identified
by scientists,
baleen whales
and toothed
whales, having
each of these
categories many
sub species.

All cetaceans have forelimbs modified as fins, a tail with horizontal flukes, and nasal openings on top of the head.

As with all mammals whales are warm-blooded, nurse their young with milk from mammary glands and have body hair.

Beneath the whales skin lies a layer of fat called blubber, which stores energy and insulates the body.

Although whales do not possess fully developed hind limbs, some possess discrete rudimentary appendages, which may contain feet and digits.

Whales have a spinal column, a vestigial pelvic bone, and a four-chambered heart. Typically, the neck vertebrae are fused, an adaptation trading flexibility for stability during swimming.

Whales generally are classed as predators. Their food ranges from microscopic plankton to very large animals.

Toothed whales eat fish and squid, which they hunt by the use of echolocation. Baleen whales, such as humpbacks and blues, mainly eat krill when feeding in the higher latitudes.

Sperm whale's have the largest brain of any creature known to have lived on Earth. The head consists of a cavity large enough to park a car inside that contains a yellowish wax called spermaceti.

The humpback whale is one of the best known baleen whale species. The humpback whale is famous for its songs, of which even records have been made.

The humpback whales that feed in Antarctic waters and swim north to breed off the coasts of Colombia, Panama and Costa Rica make one of the longest confirmed migration of any mammal.

Printed in Great Britain
by Amazon